THE OFFICIAL CELTIC ANNUAL 2026

Written by Joe Sullivan
Designed by Chris Dalrymple

A Grange Publication

Grange Communications Ltd., 25 Herbert Place, Dublin, D02 AY86
frontdesk@grangecommunications.co.uk

Printed in Romania.

Photographs by Alan Whyte and Ryan Whyte, Angus Johnston, Celtic Multi-Media, Alamy.

Special thanks to Matthew Campbell and Lewis Laird.

Double and Women's Artwork by Shaun Campbell, Robert McKenzie.

ISBN: 978-1-917538-33-6

CONT

ENTS

CLUB HONOURS

Scottish League Winners [55 times]
1892/93, 1893/94, 1895/96, 1897/98, 1904/05, 1905/06, 1906/07, 1907/08, 1908/09, 1909/10, 1913/14, 1914/15, 1915/16, 1916/17, 1918/19, 1921/22, 1925/26, 1935/36, 1937/38, 1953/54, 1965/66, 1966/67, 1967/68, 1968/69, 1969/70, 1970/71, 1971/72, 1972/73, 1973/74, 1976/77, 1978/79, 1980/81, 1981/82, 1985/86, 1987/88, 1997/98, 2000/01, 2001/02, 2003/04, 2005/06, 2006/07, 2007/08, 2011/12, 2012/13, 2013/14, 2014/15, 2015/16, 2016/17, 2017/18, 2018/19, 2019/20, 2021/22, 2022/23, 2023/24, 2024/25

Scottish Cup Winners [42 times]
1892, 1899, 1900, 1904, 1907, 1908, 1911, 1912, 1914, 1923, 1925, 1927, 1931, 1933, 1937, 1951, 1954, 1965, 1967, 1969, 1971, 1972, 1974, 1975, 1977, 1980, 1985, 1988, 1989, 1995, 2001, 2004, 2005, 2007, 2011, 2013, 2017, 2018, 2019, 2020, 2023, 2024

League Cup Winners [22 times]
1956/57, 1957/58, 1965/66, 1966/67, 1967/68, 1968/69, 1969/70, 1974/75, 1982/83, 1997/98, 1999/00, 2000/01, 2005/06, 2008/09, 2014/15, 2016/17, 2017/18, 2018/19, 2019/20, 2021/22, 2022/23, 2024/25

European Cup Winners 1967

Coronation Cup Winners 1953

BRENDAN RODGERS

WITH Brendan Rodgers at the helm, season 2024/25 was another hugely successful campaign for Celtic with the fourth title in a row and the League Cup win highlights of the year as well as there being further improvement and standing in Europe.

On a personal note for the Irishman, that League Cup win took him into double figures with trophies at Celtic as that was his 10th with the club – the same trophy that was his first success with Celtic in his first spell with the club back in 2016/17.

And that particular win back then was also the 100th major trophy the club had won, and by the end of last term, that tally stood at 120 – a measure of the amazing success in silverware that Celtic have had since Brendan Rodgers arrived in 2016 and returned once more in 2023 to take up the mantle again.

Now his personal tally stands at 11 major wins with Celtic in little more than four-and-a-half seasons, and the fact that the Hoops carried on winning in the interim was also helped by the winning tradition and belief that he instilled in the team, the club and the supporters.

However, personal tallies and accolades aren't something he takes great credit or recognition in, and he is always first to acknowledge the input of his entire coaching staff and backroom team, the players and the work they put in every single day on the training pitch at Lennoxtown, and, not least, the amazing Celtic support that have urged the side on both home and away.

No more so is the valuable input of the Celtic support displayed than in European games under the lights at Paradise, when they have driven the team on to dramatic late goals on many occasions, and in 2024/25 the crowd played their part in Brendan Rodgers' team restating Celtic's standing on the continent.

The new-look UEFA Champions League tournament pitted Celtic with some of the best teams from Germany, Italy, Belgium, England, Croatia, Slovakia and Switzerland, and they qualified for the Knockout Play-offs of the competition.

Again, after competing against both Borussia Dortmund and RB Leipzig from Germany in the League Stage of the tournament, Brendan Rodgers' Celts faced stiff Bundesliga competition once more in the qualifiers in the shape of the mighty Bayern Munich.

Celtic lost narrowly 2-1 in Glasgow after having an early goal chalked off and then had an even closer fight in the Allianz Arena in Munich when they levelled the aggregate score to 2-2 by taking a 1-0 lead, but, heartbreakingly went out in the cruellest possible way to an equaliser in the 94th minute. Nevertheless, that night and the League Stage wins and draws to get there showed just how much the team had upped their European game.

The manager had transferred that winning belief from Celtic's domestic play to the continental game, and, although we know there will be ups and downs, the team now go into European games with confidence instilled by Brendan Rodgers.

MANAGER FACTFILE

D.O.B: 26/01/73
Born: Carnlough, Ireland

PLAYING CAREER RECORD:

Ballymena United (1987-90)
Reading (1990-93)
Newport (1993-94)
Witney Town (1994-95)
Newbury Town (1995-96)

AS MANAGER:

Watford (2008-09)
Reading (2009)
Swansea City (2010-12)
Liverpool (2012-15)
Celtic (2016-19)
Leicester City (2019-23)
Celtic (2023 to date)

MANAGERIAL HONOURS:

Celtic:
League Champions (2016/17, 2017/18, 2023/24, 2024/25)
Scottish Cup Winners (2016/17, 2017/18, 2023/24)
League Cup Winners (2016/17, 2017/18, 2018/19, 2024/25)

Leicester City:
FA Cup (2020/21)
FA Community Shield (2021)

SILVER CELT

THE MEDAL COUNT OF JAMES FORREST, A TRUE CELTIC LEGEND

JUST over 10 years ago, as Celtic entered the middle years of the 2010s, the most recent addition to the Top 10 of most decorated Celts had been the legendary Danny McGrain with 14 medals for his exploits in the 1970s and '80s.

He had joined an elite band of men – no fewer than five Lisbon Lions dominated the upper echelons of that list, with other Celts of further days gone by such as Alec McNair, Jimmy McMenemy and Sunny Jim Young adding over five decades of Celtic service and experience between them to the list.

However, after 40 years with no change to the list, another era of Celtic dominance gradually introduced new names to the front runners of the most decorated Celts – Scott Brown edged above McGrain, soon followed by team-mate, Mikael Lustig and a young precocious winger named James Forrest, with another youngster called Callum McGregor not far behind.

As the successful decade progressed they made further inroads to a Top 10 dominated by the Lions and racked up the medals with Forrest and McGregor edging their way up with each passing season.

Prior to the past 10 years, it was presumed that the places of the only two Celts with over 20 medals – Bobby Lennox on 25 and Billy McNeill on 23 – were set in stone.

After all, you wouldn't only have to have over 10 years as a first-team player with the club, you would also have to be part of a very successful team, therefore making it all the more difficult to remain a first-team player – the chances seemed slim.

Last season, however, after a decade of unparalleled success for Celtic, James Forrest equalled and then overtook Bobby Lennox's half-a-century at the top of the club's medal table, as at the end of the term his League Cup and SPFL medals took him to 26 in total – an astounding achievement.

Here we take a look back at his magnificent trophy count.

JAMES FORREST MEDALLION MAN HIS ROLL OF HONOUR

League titles (13):
2011/12, 2012/13, 2013/14, 2014/15, 2015/16, 2016/17, 2017/18, 2018/19, 2019/20, 2021/22, 2022/23, 2023/24, 2024/25.

Scottish Cups (7):
2010/11, 2012/13, 2016/17, 2017/18, 2018/19, 2022/23, 2023/24.

Scottish League Cups (6):
2014/15, 2016/17, 2017/18, 2018/19, 2019/20, 2024/25.

After every 20.3 Celtic games, somebody has handed James Forrest a winner's medal.

After every 15.8 Celtic domestic games, somebody has handed James Forrest a winner's medal.

ALL-TIME TOP CELTIC MEDAL WINNERS

Player	League	Scottish Cup	League Cup	Europe	Total
James Forrest	**13**	**7**	**6**		**26**
Bobby Lennox	11	8	5	1	25
Callum McGregor	**10**	**6**	**8**		**24**
Billy McNeill	9	7	6	1	23
Scott Brown	10	6	6		22
Jimmy Johnstone	9	4	5	1	19
Bobby Murdoch	8	4	5	1	18
Alec McNair	12	6			18
Jimmy McMenemy	11	7			18
Mikael Lustig	8	4	4		16

LISBON LION UNFURLS THE COLOURS

JIM CRAIG FLIES THE FLAG FOR THE CHAMPIONS

OVER 50 years ago, Flag Days weren't what they are now. Back then, a rather stylish car such as a Rolls Royce or Bentley would appear on the track and drive around the pitch to the space between The Jungle and the East Terracing.

Out of the car would come a few dignitaries, then the wife of a director or maybe Mrs Stein would raise a green and white saltire to fly atop a flagpole, and that was it.

It was all so very dated, very 1940s never mind 1970s. However, if the Flag Day celebrations back in the '60s and '70s were more in line with today's festivities, then Jim Craig would have experienced a good few of them, and on a yearly basis.

The Lisbon Lion was on hand at the start of last season to do the honours with title flag, and, did so surrounded by a colourful full-stadium display after club captain, Callum McGregor carried out the trophy before the Hoops marked the day by beating Kilmarnock 4-0.

And like club legend, Jim Craig and his '60s and '70s team-mates, the Celts of recent years have had a happy habit of winning consecutive titles to give the fans the best possible way to start and finish the league campaign – with the raising of the colours before the first game, and the raising of the trophy after the last game.

AUGUST

FOLLOWING a pre-season trip to the States and scoring four goals in each of the games against DC United (4-0), Manchester City (4-3) and Chelsea (4-1), season 2024/25 began by celebrating the fruits of 2023/24 as Lisbon Lion, Jim Craig unfurled the colours on Flag Day, and the current Celts responded in the best possible manner with a 4-0 win over Kilmarnock.

The honour of scoring the first goal of the new term fell to Reo Hatate as he buried a shot from the edge of the area in the 17th minute.

Liam Scales added another before the break, while Nicolas Kühn and Anthony Ralston did likewise in the second half as the Celts started their defence of the trophy in the way they meant to go on.

The first away destination for the Hoops was Easter Road where Hibernian lay in wait at the start of a double-header that would see the same two teams meet the following weekend in the League Cup at Celtic Park.

Before the 20-minute mark, the champions were 2-0 ahead, with Kühn keeping up his scoring record while Callum McGregor also got in on the act with a long-range effort.

The game finished on that 2-0 scoreline as the sides got ready to face-off again the following Sunday, and two goals inside the first 17 minutes by Daizen Maeda put the Hoops in the driving seat.

Hibs did pull one back, but Kühn again maintained his deadliness in front of goal and the Celts went through to the quarter-finals with a 3-1 win.

The opening month finished with a trip to Paisley and a 3-0 win over St Mirren thanks to goals from McGregor, again from outside the box, Hatate and Alistair Johnston.

TRANSFER TALES

Some of the transfer window movement was completed in July, allowing the likes of Kasper Schmeichel and Viljami Sinisalo to travel to the games in the States, but they were joined by other new faces such as Arne Engels, Auston Trusty and Luke McCowan, while Paulo Bernardo and Adam Idah signed permanently after being on loan in the second half of the previous term. Matt O'Riley was the biggest of the names who moved in the other direction, while others were Oh, Tomoki, Mikey Johnston and Ben Siegrist.

THE MATCHES

Comp	Venue	Date	Opposition	Score	Scorers
SPFL	H	Sun 04	Kilmarnock	4-0	Hatate 17, Scales 40, Kühn 59, Ralston 90+4
SPFL	A	Sun 11	Hibernian	2-0	Kühn 3, McGregor 19
LC	H	Sun 18	Hibernian	3-1	Maeda 4, 15, Kühn 56
SPFL	A	Sun 25	St Mirren	3-0	McGregor 3, Hatate 33, Johnston 71

TABLE-TOP

	P	W	D	L	F	A	GD	Pts
1 Aberdeen	4	4	0	0	8	2	6	12
2 CELTIC	**3**	**3**	**0**	**0**	**9**	**0**	**9**	**9**
3 Rangers	3	2	1	0	8	1	7	7

SEPTEMBER

IN any month you would take five wins out of five with 21 goals scored and only three goals against (none of them in the SPFL) – but when that month includes a derby, a UEFA Champions League game and a League Cup quarter-final, you know it was pretty memorable.

September began in the best possible way with a derby win as the Ibrox side arrived for the final game before an international break with the Celts already five points above their city rivals.

As the first half progressed there was little doubt that the gap would be eight points after just four games played, as Daizen Maeda opened the scoring in the 17th minute and his Japanese counterpart, Kyogo made it 2-0 before the break.

In the second half, skipper, Callum McGregor scored another screamer from outside the box and the 3-0 win was more than justified.

Following the international break, Hearts arrived at Paradise, and it was now time for the new Bhoys to take up the mantle, as midfielders, Arne Engels, from the spot, and Luke McCowan netted their first goals for the club in a 2-0 win over the Edinburgh side.

Next came two cup games, the first of those being Celtic's bow in the new UCL set-up with the visit of Slovakian outfit, Slovan Bratislava as the Hoops delivered a football masterclass.

Five different scorers helped the Celts to a 5-1 win to kick-off a European campaign with plenty of promise.

Falkirk then arrived on League Cup duty and the Championship side took the lead not once, but twice and went into the break 2-1 ahead with their goals sandwiching a Paulo Bernardo equaliser.

In a 14-minute spell of the second half, though, doubles from Adam Idah and Nicolas Kühn took the final score to 5-2.

The final game of September was an away trip to play St Johnstone at McDiarmid Park, and the flawless start to the league campaign continued with a 6-0 win, including the obligatory McGregor long-ranger, taking the champions to 20 league goals scored with none against.

THE MATCHES

Comp	Venue	Date	Opposition	Score	Scorers
SPFL	H	Sun 01	Rangers	3-0	Maeda 17, Kyogo 40, McGregor 75
SPFL	H	Sat 14	Hearts	2-0	Engels pen 52, McCowan 89
UCL	H	Wed 18	Slovan Bratislava	5-1	Scales 17, Kyogo 47, Engels 56 pen, Maeda 70, Idah 86
LC	H	Sun 22	Falkirk	5-2	Bernardo 21, Idah 70, 72, Kühn 81, 84
SPFL	A	Sat 28	St Johnstone	6-0	Kyogo 35, 45, Bernardo 43, McGregor 54, Maeda 72, Idah 83

TABLE-TOP

	P	W	D	L	F	A	GD	Pts
1 CELTIC	**6**	**6**	**0**	**0**	**20**	**0**	**20**	**18**
2 Aberdeen	6	6	0	0	12	4	8	18
3 Rangers	6	3	1	2	10	4	6	13

OCTOBER

THIS month saw the tale of two UEFA Champions League games – one that showed the Celts what they were up against, and the other which illustrated what they could do and gave them the belief that this was a stage where they belonged.

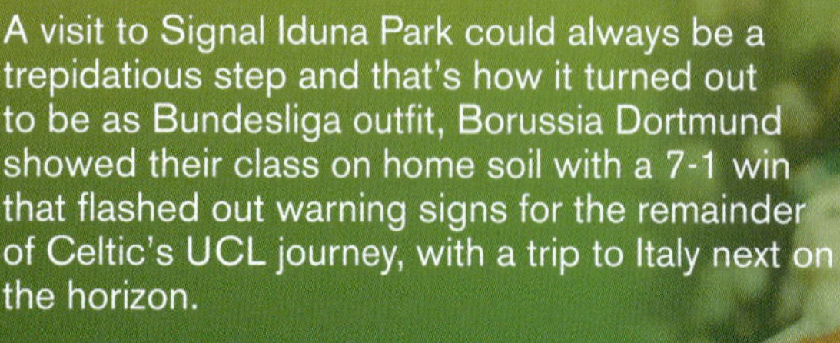

A visit to Signal Iduna Park could always be a trepidatious step and that's how it turned out to be as Bundesliga outfit, Borussia Dortmund showed their class on home soil with a 7-1 win that flashed out warning signs for the remainder of Celtic's UCL journey, with a trip to Italy next on the horizon.

Three weeks later, the Hoops travelled to Bergamo to take on Serie A side, Atalanta, and a resolute performance not only delivered a well-earned point in this 0-0 game but helped instil the conviction to win other points in games yet to come.

In between the two UCL games were a pair of SPFL outings, first a 2-1 win at Ross County after the home side had taken the lead from the spot.

Then came one of the most anticipated non-derby league games in years as Celtic and Aberdeen faced off with only a better goal difference keeping the Hoops on top.

At the end of the game, the same goal difference stood despite Celtic taking an early two-goal lead as a couple of slips at the back saw Aberdeen score twice in a 10-minute period for a 2-2 draw.

The month ended with two league games in quick succession as a short trip to Motherwell saw the Hoops return with all three points after a 3-0 win, then Dundee visited for a midweek clash, and goals from Alistair Johnston, his second in consecutive games, and Arne Engels kept Celtic's championship defence intact.

THE MATCHES

Comp	Venue	Date	Opposition	Score	Scorers
UCL	A	Tue 01	Borussia Dortmund	1-7	Maeda 9
SPFL	A	Sun 06	Ross County	2-1	Johnston 76, Kühn 88
SPFL	H	Sat 19	Aberdeen	2-2	Hatate 24, Kyogo 27
UCL	A	Wed 23	Atalanta	0-0	
SPFL	A	Sun 27	Motherwell	3-0	McCowan 27, Johnston 56, Idah 88
SPFL	H	Wed 30	Dundee	2-0	Johnston 60, Engels 67 pen

TABLE-TOP

	P	W	D	L	F	A	GD	Pts
1 CELTIC	**10**	**9**	**1**	**0**	**29**	**3**	**26**	**28**
2 Aberdeen	10	9	1	0	20	9	11	28
3 Rangers	10	6	1	3	15	8	7	10

NOVEMBER

THE first working week of the month threw up three tests that Celtic would do well to come out of unscathed – that they did so by displaying three different facets of their game-plan speaks volumes for the confidence and belief that Brendan Rodgers instilled in the group.

Aberdeen in the League Cup semi-final, RB Leipzig in the UCL and a stuffy Kilmarnock side on their own difficult surface would have shaken the foundation of other sides – the Celts didn't even wobble.

First up was Aberdeen at Hampden, the team who had gone neck and neck with Celtic all season in the league, but a devastating display blew the opposition apart with a 6-0 win.

It would be sheer conjecture to suggest that this League Cup performance and goal-fest derailed Aberdeen's league title challenge, but their results in the weeks after Hampden wouldn't imply otherwise.

In midweek, despite Bundesliga side RB Leipzig taking the lead midway through the first half, the Celts on the pitch soaked up the atmosphere created by the Celts off the pitch and, amid one of the most memorable European nights at Paradise, a 3-1 win for the Hoops was lauded far beyond the confines of the stadium.

Next was the sticky surface at Rugby Park where the Celts had their moments the previous term, but another Callum McGregor out-of-the-area delivery opened the scoring, although this one was more down to trajectory rather than velocity. Then Nicolas Kühn scored the other in the 2-0 win – his fourth goal of the three-game week.

After another international break, despite facing another traditionally difficult away trip, this time to Tynecastle, the Celts were on the money again, and so was Kühn who kept up his run by netting the second goal in a 4-1 win over Hearts.

Hot on the heels of that was another UCL test and this time a stylish strike from Daizen Maeda earned another well-won vital point in a 1-1 draw with the Belgian champions, Club Brugge.

And the curtain was brought down on November with five different first-half scorers delivering a 5-0 win over Ross County.

THE MATCHES

Comp	Venue	Date	Opposition	Score	Scorers
LC	N	Sat 02	Aberdeen	6-0	Carter-Vickers 29, Kyogo 32, Maeda 40, 49, 85, Kühn 59
UCL	H	Tue 05	RB Leipzig	3-1	Kühn 35, 45+1, Hatate 72
SPFL	A	Sun 10	Kilmarnock	2-0	McGregor 45+4, Kühn 71
SPFL	A	Sat 23	Hearts	4-1	Kyogo 55, Kühn 60, Idah 78, 90+4 pen
UCL	H	Wed 27	Club Brugge	1-1	Maeda 60
SPFL	H	Sat 30	Ross County	5-0	Scales 10, McCowan 27, Bernardo 35, McGregor 36, Idah 40

TABLE-TOP

	P	W	D	L	F	A	GD	Pts
1 CELTIC	**13**	**12**	**1**	**0**	**40**	**4**	**36**	**37**
2 Aberdeen	13	10	2	1	28	15	13	32
3 Rangers	12	7	2	3	17	9	8	23

DECEMBER

THE headline for the month of December was, of course, the League Cup final triumph at Hampden as Brendan Rodgers' side picked up the first silverware of the 2024/25 season and reclaimed the only trophy which evaded them the previous year.

That success came at the end of a pulsating final, with the Hoops coming from behind twice to lead in the game, only to be pegged back on both occasions. Celtic's scorers on the day were Greg Taylor, Daizen Maeda and Nicolas Kühn.

It meant that, after 120 minutes of action and with the game tied at 3-3, the destiny of the cup would be decided by a penalty shoot-out.

Adam Idah, Callum McGregor, Arne Engels and Reo Hatate all converted their spot-kicks, while Kasper Schmeichel saved one of Rangers' efforts, giving Daizen Maeda the opportunity to win the cup for Celtic, which he duly did.

It was Celtic's 22nd success in the competition and Brendan Rodgers' 10th trophy as Celtic manager.

Like the previous month's fixtures, December had started off with a game against Aberdeen, this time at Pittodrie and the team who hadn't lost at home in the league hosted the team who had won all of their away games.

Something had to give, and Aberdeen gave way when a Reo Hatate shot rustled the back of the net in the 78th minute on a night of foul weather to give Celtic a 1-0 win to remain the only unbeaten team in the league.

A few days later, Hibernian arrived at Celtic Park, and three goals delivered three points and three wins over the Easter Road side so far that term.

The Hoops were also in European action and gained another valuable away point following a 0-0 draw in Croatia against Dinamo Zagreb, to put the team in a strong position for further progress in the UEFA Champions League with two games remaining.

Back in the SPFL, there was a slight blip with a 0-0 draw against Dundee United at Tannadice, before eight goals were split nicely between the next two home matches to finish the year.

First up were Motherwell followed by St Johnstone in the final game of a memorable calendar year. Both games followed similar patterns with the Hoops leading 1-0 at half-time and adding three goals in the second half of each game.

THE MATCHES

Comp	Venue	Date	Opposition	Score	Scorers
SPFL	A	Wed 04	Aberdeen	1-0	Hatate 78
SPFL	H	Sat 07	Hibernian	3-0	Engels 6, Newell 54 og, Kyogo 84
UCL	A	Tue 10	Dinamo Zagreb	0-0	
LC	N	Sun 15	Rangers	3-3*	Taylor 56, Maeda 60, Kühn 87
SPFL	A	Sun 22	Dundee United	0-0	
SPFL	H	Thu 26	Motherwell	4-0	Engels 45+1 pen, Maeda 57, Kühn 74, Hatate 81
SPFL	H	Sun 29	St Johnstone	4-0	Kühn 30, Kyogo 59, 64, Maeda 73

* Celtic won the League Cup final 5-4 on penalties

TABLE-TOP

	P	W	D	L	F	A	GD	Pts
1 CELTIC	**18**	**16**	**2**	**0**	**52**	**4**	**48**	**50**
2 Rangers	18	11	3	4	31	13	18	36
3 Aberdeen	19	10	4	5	31	25	5	34

JANUARY

WITH no winter break, January was a busy month with no fewer than eight games played in what had normally been a quieter month in previous seasons.

It didn't get off to the best possible start as a defeat at Ibrox heralded the beginning of the year for the Hoops.

However, they soon got back on track just three days later when another brace from German winger, Nicolas Kühn sandwiched a first goal in the Hoops for Auston Trusty with the Celts beating St Mirren 3-0 in the East End of Glasgow.

The success continued in the third game of the week when Dundee United, who had held Celtic to a 0-0 draw just a little over a fortnight earlier were beaten 2-0 with the Japanese duo of Daizen Maeda and Reo Hatate accounting for the goals.

There was another quick turnaround, though, as a few days later there was a trip north to play Ross County, and, despite the home side equalising on the hour mark after Kyogo gave Celtic a first-half lead, the Japanese striker struck again in the 81st minute. Goals late in the game from Arne Engels and Luke McCowan delivered a 4-1 win.

There were even more goals scored in the next game, but they were divided equally between both teams as Celtic and Dundee fought out a 3-3 draw at Dens Park with a 93rd-minute penalty by Engels saving the point.

SPFL action was put to the side as the remaining three games of the month featured the Scottish Cup and the Champions League. Callum McGregor opened with a belter of a goal against Kilmarnock, and, although the visitors equalised just before the break, Daizen Maeda made sure of the 2-1 win in the second half.

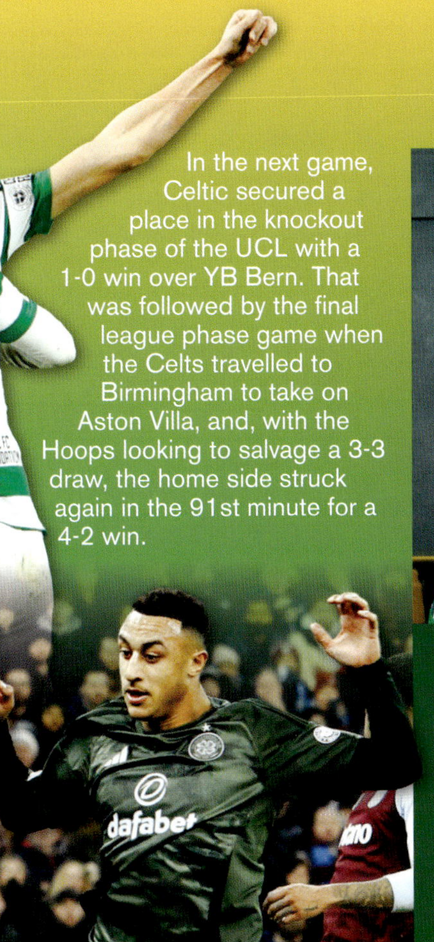

In the next game, Celtic secured a place in the knockout phase of the UCL with a 1-0 win over YB Bern. That was followed by the final league phase game when the Celts travelled to Birmingham to take on Aston Villa, and, with the Hoops looking to salvage a 3-3 draw, the home side struck again in the 91st minute for a 4-2 win.

TRANSFER TALES

On the transfer front, the window ended with a couple of moves, one of those being Luis Palma who moved out on loan to Greek side Olympiacos. The big news, however, saw two big Celtic stars of recent years move in the opposite direction to each other as Kyogo moved to French side Rennes, while Jota left the French club to come back to Celtic a year-and-a-half after joining Al-Ittihad in Saudi Arabia. Jota had scored 28 goals in 83 games for Celtic in his first spell with the club, and the January switch was welcomed as a great coup by the Hoops support.

THE MATCHES

Comp	Venue	Date	Opposition	Score	Scorers
SPFL	A	Thu 02	Rangers	0-3	
SPFL	H	Sat 05	St Mirren	3-0	Kühn 33, 68, Trusty 43
SPFL	H	Wed 08	Dundee United	2-0	Maeda 22, Hatate 83
SPFL	A	Sat 11	Ross County	4-1	Kyogo 40, 81, Engels 90+6, McCowan 90+8
SPFL	A	Tue 14	Dundee	3-3	McCowan 5, Yang 53, Engels 90+3 pen
SC	H	Sat 18	Kilmarnock	2-1	McGregor 12, Maeda 70
UCL	H	Wed 22	YB Bern	1-0	Benito 85 og
UCL	A	Wed 29	Aston Villa	2-4	Idah 36, 38

TABLE-TOP

	P	W	D	L	F	A	GD	Pts
1 CELTIC	**23**	**19**	**3**	**1**	**64**	**11**	**53**	**60**
2 Rangers	24	15	5	4	47	19	28	50
3 Dundee Utd	24	10	7	7	32	27	5	37

FEBRUARY

ON the domestic front, the Hoops had games in both the league and the Scottish Cup to take care of, but there was also the big attraction of the play-off round of the new-look UEFA Champions League.

The formidable challenge of German giants, Bayern Munich stood between the Celts and progression in the tournament, and, although the Bundesliga side narrowly took the honours, there were obvious signs that the Celts had made progress in their European intentions – headway that was noted all over the continent.

A flagged-off goal in the first 30 seconds by Nicolas Kühn showed Celtic's intent, but goals either side of the break gave Bayern a 2-0 lead before Daizen Maeda pulled one back to give the Hoops hope on their trip to the Allianz a week later.

Once more the Celts excelled on the European stage, and Kühn did get that goal against his former club when he put the Hoops ahead in the 63rd minute to make it 2-2 on aggregate.

Heartbreakingly, though, when the Celts thought they had at least forced the tie to extra-time, the home side equalised in the 94th minute with the last kick of the game.

Celtic's performances, though, gained plaudits all over Europe as their reputation on the continent took great strides forward.

Prior to the first Bayern match, comeback Bhoy, Jota got the third in a 3-1 league win at Motherwell, while there were four scorers in a 6-0 win over Dundee, and that was followed by a 5-0 win in the Scottish Cup over Raith Rovers.

Between the Bayern games was a 3-0 win over Dundee United while a controversial 2-1 defeat at Easter Road was only Celtic's second defeat of the league campaign so far.

The Celts bounced back just a few days later, though, with a 5-1 win over Aberdeen to end the month on a high with a 13-point lead at the top.

THE MATCHES

Comp	Venue	Date	Opposition	Score	Scorers
SPFL	A	Sun 02	Motherwell	3-1	Maeda 1, Idah 29, Jota 90+4
SPFL	H	Wed 05	Dundee	6-0	Engels 18 pen, 71, Idah 45+1, Maeda 55, 59, Kühn 81
SC	H	Sat 08	Raith Rovers	5-0	Maeda 6, 45+3, 77, McCowan 47, Yang 56
UCL	H	Wed 12	Bayern Munich	1-2	Maeda 79
SPFL	H	Sat 15	Dundee United	3-0	McGregor 23, Jota 35, Idah 84
UCL	A	Wed 18	Bayern Munich	1-1	Kühn 63
SPFL	A	Sat 22	Hibernian	1-2	Maeda 68
SPFL	H	Tue 25	Aberdeen	5-1	Maeda 24, 90+2, Jota 30, McGregor 45, Yang 72

TABLE-TOP

	P	W	D	L	F	A	GD	Pts
1 CELTIC	**28**	**23**	**3**	**2**	**82**	**15**	**67**	**72**
2 Rangers	28	18	5	5	58	24	34	59
3 Aberdeen	28	12	5	11	36	44	-8	41

MARCH

A REASONABLY quiet month games-wise with an international break meaning only four games over the course of March.

One of those games, though, was a derby against Rangers, and, true to form, there was nothing quiet about this game.

It was the third game of the month and the final match before breaking up for the international matches, and the visitors had a 2-0 half-time lead before the Japanese double act of Daizen Maeda and Reo Hatate made it 2-2 by the 74th minute.

That's the way it stood until the 88th minute when an unfortunate slip on the turf allowed the visitors a chance to score and take the game 3-2.

The month started, though, with a 5-2 win over St Mirren in Paisley in a game that featured Jeffrey Schlupp's first goal for the club when he scored the opener in the 28th minute.

The game also featured another goal from Daizen Maeda who would score in every game this month amid a tally of eight goals in six consecutive games for the Celts.

Among that run was his opener in the next game, a 2-0 win over Hibernian and, of course, the Japanese hitman maintained his sequence in the next game against Rangers.

Returning from the international break, Maeda netted a double, sandwiching another goal from Jota, as the Hoops beat Hearts 3-0, and, despite that derby slip-up, results elsewhere saw the champions still finish the month the same 13 points ahead at the top.

THE MATCHES

Comp	Venue	Date	Opposition	Score	Scorers
SPFL	A	Sat 01	St Mirren	5-2	Schlupp 28, Engels 45+1 pen, Maeda 88, Yang 68, 90+3
SC	H	Sun 09	Hibernian	2-0	Maeda 39, Idah 90+2
SPFL	H	Sun 16	Rangers	2-3	Maeda 49, Hatate 74
SPFL	H	Sat 29	Hearts	3-0	Maeda 17, 41, Jota 24

TABLE-TOP

	P	W	D	L	F	A	GD	Pts
1 CELTIC	**31**	**25**	**3**	**3**	**92**	**20**	**72**	**78**
2 Rangers	31	20	5	6	66	31	35	65
3 Hibernian	31	12	11	8	48	41	7	47

APRIL

DESPITE starting off with a surprising defeat, Celtic's lead at the top of the table increased from 13 points to 17 over the month of April, but, rather more importantly, the last of those points ensured that the Hoops were uncatchable – yes, the Bhoys were Champions again with their 55th title.

In the run-up to that title-clincher, Celtic suffered that shock 1-0 defeat to bottom club St Johnstone at McDiarmid Park that meant they now couldn't definitively clinch the league in the next game against Kilmarnock at Paradise in front of an expectant home crowd.

Still, on the day, the Celts didn't let that disappointment hold them back, and delivered a 5-1 win before meeting St Johnstone again, this time in the Scottish Cup.

There was no shock from the Saints this time at Hampden as four goals in the first half were added to by another after the break for another five-goal performance that took the Hoops through to the Scottish Cup final.

That left the final game of the month, and one in which the Hoops could seal the title in the first match following the league split, as Dundee United awaited at Tannadice in an early lunchtime kick-off.

By half-time the title was basically Celtic's with the Hoops having a three-goal lead, and, by the hour mark, that lead had stretched to five goals and that 5-0 scoreline was the final result.

The final whistle may have stopped play but it kicked off celebration parties for Celts around the world – and no more so than on the pitch at Tannadice as the players and fans saluted each other on the taking of a fourth successive title.

THE MATCHES

Comp	Venue	Date	Opposition	Score	Scorers
SPFL	A	Sun 06	St Johnstone	0-1	
SPFL	H	Sat 12	Kilmarnock	5-1	Hatate 9, 24, Maeda 11, Carter-Vickers 21, Ralston 90+3
SC	N	Sun 20	St Johnstone	5-0	McGregor 34, Maeda 37, 45+1, Idah 45, Jota 67
SPFL	A	Sat 26	Dundee United	5-0	Strain og 30, Kühn 38, 45+3, Idah 47, 58

TABLE-TOP

	P	W	D	L	F	A	GD	Pts
1 CELTIC	**34**	**27**	**3**	**4**	**102**	**22**	**80**	**84**
2 Rangers	34	20	7	7	70	37	33	67
3 Hibernian	34	14	11	9	54	21	12	53

MAY

THE final two games of the term finished 1-1, with one lauded as a fantastic victory and the other lamented as a defeat, but it was still another history-making season for Celtic with silverware in the shape of the League Cup and the SPFL title taking the tally to 120 major trophies.

However, before the euphoria and anguish at the end of the month, May also started with a 1-1 draw, this time at Ibrox – a result that was also celebrated under the circumstances with Adam Idah equalising for the newly-crowned Champions.

A 3-1 win over Hibernian followed, then a few days later, fellow Scottish Cup finalists, Aberdeen were defeated 5-1 by a greatly changed Celtic side with young Irishman, Johnny Kenny scoring his first goal for the club as the Hoops readied themselves for another Trophy Day at Paradise ahead of the Scottish Cup final.

With Jota and Reo Hatate missing through injury, that final wasn't what we hoped for, with both sides scoring own goals and both the regulation time and extra time finishing 1-1, making way for a penalty shoot-out that Aberdeen won 4-3.

The other 1-1 draw, though, came on the seemingly customary Trophy Day at Celtic Park to bring the curtain down on yet another successful league season for the Celts, and you can read more about that by turning over the page.

THE MATCHES

Comp	Venue	Date	Opposition	Score	Scorers
SPFL	A	Sun 04	Rangers	1-1	Idah 57
SPFL	H	Sat 10	Hibernian	3-1	Kühn 41, Idah 45, Hatate 58
SPFL	A	Wed 14	Aberdeen	5-1	Nawrocki 31, Yang 45+8, McCowan 48, Kenny 54, Idah 90+4
SPFL	H	Sat 17	St Mirren	1-1	Forrest 90+4
SC	N	Sat 24	Aberdeen	1-1	Dorrington og 39 (Aberdeen win 4-3 on penalties)

TABLE-TOP

	P	W	D	L	F	A	GD	Pts
1 CELTIC	**38**	**29**	**5**	**4**	**112**	**26**	**86**	**92**
2 Rangers	38	22	9	7	80	41	39	71
3 Hibernian	33	15	13	10	62	50	12	58

STYLE, SUNSHINE AND SILVER

ANOTHER CELTIC TROPHY DAY IN PARADISE

THE atmosphere was pumped up as Brendan Rodgers carried the SPFL Trophy up The Celtic Way with the cheers of the gathered Hoops fans adding to the expectation of the day.

The volume intensified around a few hours later as the shimmering trophy appeared again at the mouth of the tunnel, carried by James Forrest who just before that had been responsible for the decibels rattling the rafters when he produced the climax to a season-long story that saw Celtic retain the title.

Over the course of the season the winger had become Celtic's most decorated player ever with 26 winner's medals, taking over from fellow Ayrshire Celt, the legendary Lisbon Lion that is Bobby Lennox.

Another achievement was also within his grasp during the 2024/25 season, the chance to score in 16 successive seasons for Celtic, but it had eluded him in each of his games, and, with time running out, it looked like the feat had slipped from his grasp.

Even in the last league game of the season, Jamesy was listed as a sub, therefore limiting his opportunity to achieve his dream on what was set to be party day for Celtic no matter what.

St Mirren looked like they would put a damper on the party, though, when they took the lead in the 51st minute.

Just three minutes later, Forrest was sent on, but despite constant assaults on the St Mirren goal by the Celtic attack, their goal seemed to lead a charmed life – or it did until the 94th minute of the game with the seconds seemingly passing faster and faster.

Then the ball fell to Alistair Johnston as he teed up for a shot, but spotted the Hoops of James Forrest to his right, and opted for the pass – with one touch that swept the ball past the keeper into the net, the winger not only ensured Celtic didn't finish with a defeat, but, in the last minute of the last league game of the season with the last kick of the ball, he sealed that 16-season scoring feat in the best possible manner.

Celtic Park erupted and the party really began, as, for the 19th time in 25 years, a Celtic captain raised aloft the silverware of Champions.

42

CALLUM McGREGOR

Position: Midfielder
D.O.B: 14/06/1993
Born: Glasgow, Scotland
Signed: 07/07/2009
Debut: v KR Reykjavik (a) 1-0, (UCL) 15/07/2014

49

JAMES FORREST

Position: Winger
D.O.B: 07/07/1991
Born: Prestwick, Scotland
Signed: 01/07/2009
Debut: v Motherwell (h) 4-0, (SPL) 01/05/2010

56

ANTHONY RALSTON

Position: Defender
D.O.B: 16/11/1998
Born: Bellshill, Scotland
Signed: 16/11/2008
Debut: v St Johnstone (a) 1-2, (SPFL) 11/05/2016

06

AUSTON TRUSTY

Position: Defender
D.O.B: 12/08/1998
Born: Media, USA
Signed: 30/08/2024
Debut: v Slovan Bratislava (h) 5-1, (UCL) 18/09/2024

14

LUKE McCOWAN

Position: Midfielder
D.O.B: 09/12/1997
Born: Greenock, Scotland
Signed: 30/08/2024
Debut: v Rangers (h) 3-0, (SPFL) 01/09/2024

07

JOTA

Position: Forward
D.O.B: 30/03/1999
Born: Lisbon, Portugal
Signed: 01/07/22 & 27/01/25
Debut: v Ross County (h) 3-0, (LC) 23/09/2021

27

ARNE ENGELS

Position: Midfielder
D.O.B: 08/09/2003
Born: Dendermonde, Belgium
Signed: 30/08/2024
Debut: v Rangers (h) 3-0, (SPFL) 01/09/2024

63

KIERAN TIERNEY

Position: Defender
D.O.B: 05/06/1997
Born: Douglas, Isle of Man
Signed: 01/07/13 & 10/06/25
Debut: v Dundee (a) 2-1, (SPFL) 22/04/2015

41

REO HATATE

Position: Midfielder
D.O.B: 21/11/1997
Born: Suzuka, Mie, Japan
Signed: 01/01/2022
Debut: v Hibernian (h) 2-0, (SPFL) 17/01/2022

05

LIAM SCALES
Position: Defender
D.O.B: 08/08/1998
Born: Barndarrig, Ireland
Signed: 27/08/2021
Debut: v Raith Rovers (h) 3-0, (LC) 23/09/2021

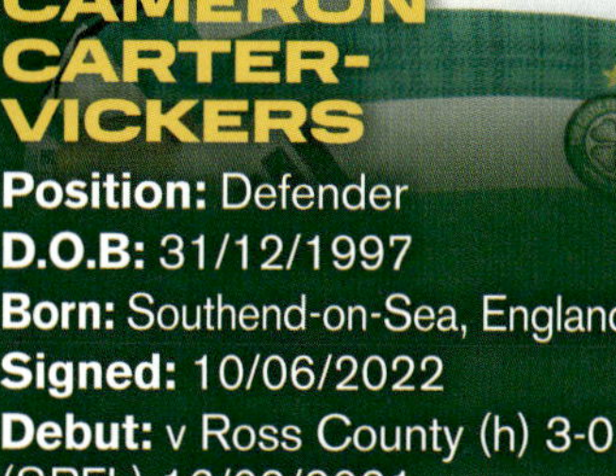

20

CAMERON CARTER-VICKERS
Position: Defender
D.O.B: 31/12/1997
Born: Southend-on-Sea, England
Signed: 10/06/2022
Debut: v Ross County (h) 3-0, (SPFL) 16/09/2021

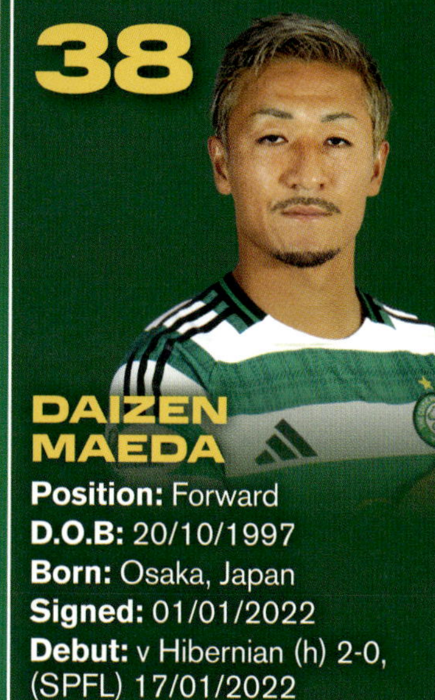

38

DAIZEN MAEDA
Position: Forward
D.O.B: 20/10/1997
Born: Osaka, Japan
Signed: 01/01/2022
Debut: v Hibernian (h) 2-0, (SPFL) 17/01/2022

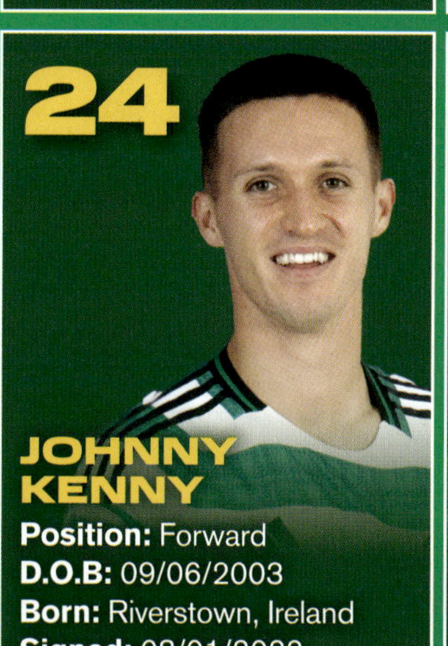

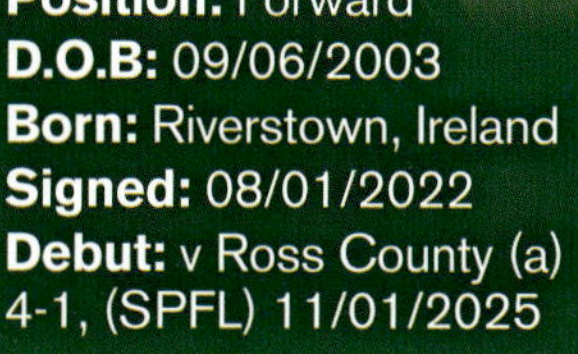

24

JOHNNY KENNY
Position: Forward
D.O.B: 09/06/2003
Born: Riverstown, Ireland
Signed: 08/01/2022
Debut: v Ross County (a) 4-1, (SPFL) 11/01/2025

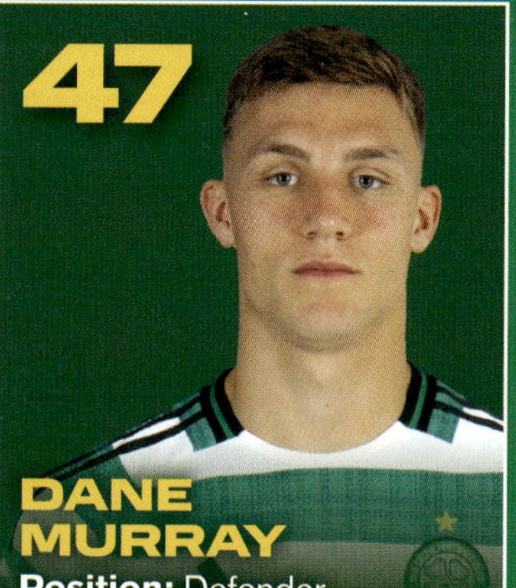

47

DANE MURRAY
Position: Defender
D.O.B: 26/06/2003
Born: Airdrie, Scotland
Signed: 01/06/2019
Debut: v FC Midtjylland (h) 1-1, (CL) 20/07/2021

02

ALISTAIR JOHNSTON
Position: Defender
D.O.B: 08/10/1998
Born: Vancouver, Canada
Signed: 03/12/2022
Debut: v Rangers (a) 2-2, (SPFL) 02/01/2023

13

HYUNJUN YANG
Position: Midfielder
D.O.B: 25/05/2002
Born: Busan, South Korea
Signed: 26/07/2023
Debut: v Ross County (h) 4-2, (SPFL) 05/08/2023

28

PAULO BERNARDO
Position: Midfielder
D.O.B: 24/01/2002
Born: Almada, Portugal
Signed: 01/08/2024
Debut: v Dundee (h) 3-0, (SPFL) 16/09/2023

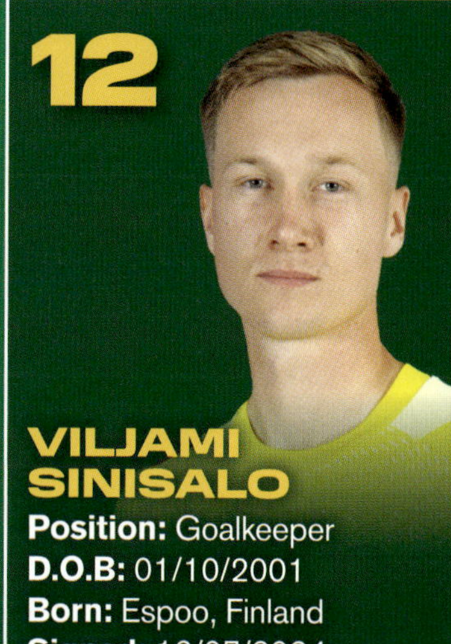

12

VILJAMI SINISALO
Position: Goalkeeper
D.O.B: 01/10/2001
Born: Espoo, Finland
Signed: 16/07/2024
Debut: v Hearts (h) 3-0, (SPFL) 29/03/2025

01

KASPER SCHMEICHEL
Position: Goalkeeper
D.O.B: 05/11/1986
Born: Copenhagen, Denmark
Signed: 18/07/2024
Debut: v Kilmarnock (h) 4-0, (SPFL) 04/08/2024

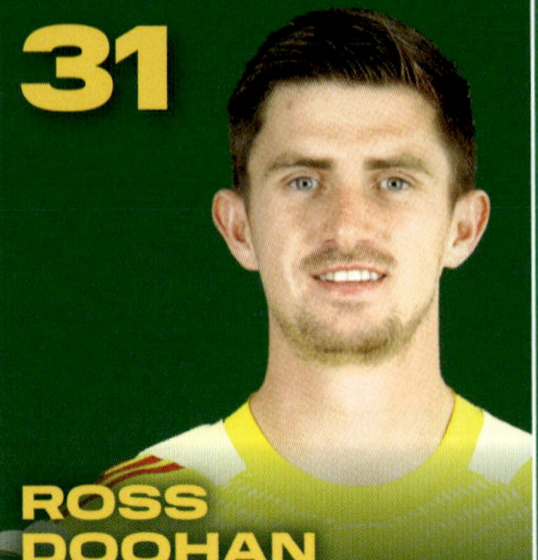

31

ROSS DOOHAN
Position: Goalkeeper
D.O.B: 29/03/1998
Born: Clydebank, Scotland
Signed: 20/06/2025
Debut: n/a

08

BENJAMIN NYGREN
Position: Forward
D.O.B: 08/07/2001
Born: Gothenburg, Sweden
Signed: 27/06/2025
Debut: v St Mirren (h) 1-0, (SPFL) 03/08/2025

19

CALLUM OSMAND
Position: Forward
D.O.B: 08/11/2005
Born: Jersey, Channel Islands
Signed: 30/06/2025
Debut: n/a

25

HAYATO INAMURA
Position: Defender
D.O.B: 06/05/2002
Born: Tokyo, Japan
Signed: 04/07/2025
Debut: v Livingston (h) 3-0 23/08/2025

18

SHIN YAMADA
Position: Forward
D.O.B: 30/05/2000
Born: Kanagawa, Japan
Signed: 19/07/2025
Debut: v Falkirk (h) 4-1 15/08/2025

04

JAHMAI SIMPSON-PUSEY
Position: Defender
D.O.B: 04/11/2005
Born: Huddersfield, England
Signed: 05/08/2025
Debut: n/a

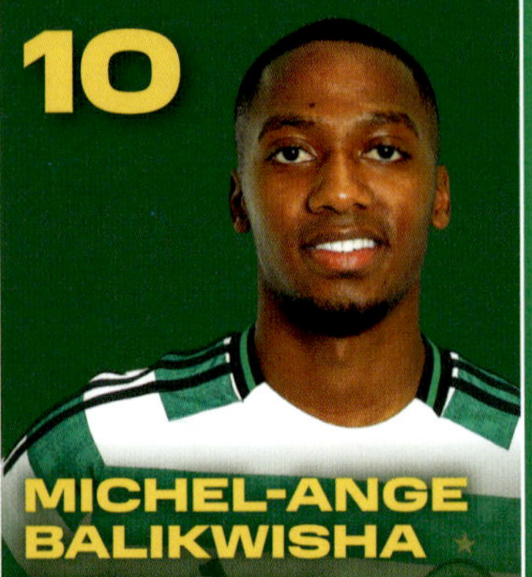

10

MICHEL-ANGE BALIKWISHA
Position: Forward
D.O.B: 10/05/2001
Born: Ghent, Belgium
Signed: 28/08/25
Debut: v Rangers (a) 0-0 (SPFL) 31/08/2025

23

SEBASTIAN TOUNEKTI
Position: Forward
D.O.B: 13/07/2002
Born: Tromso, Norway
Signed: 01/09/2025
Debut: n/a

17

KELECHI IHEANACHO

Position: Forward
D.O.B: 03/10/96
Born: Owerri, Nigeria
Signed: 02/09/25
Debut: n/a

36

MARCELO SARACCHI

Position: Defender
D.O.B: 23/04/98
Born: Paysandu, Uruguay
Signed: 28/08/25
Debut: v Rangers (a) 0-0 (SPFL) 30/08/25

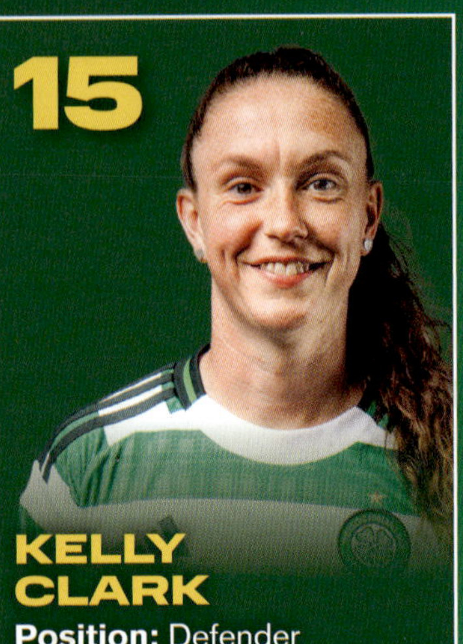

KELLY CLARK
Position: Defender
D.O.B: 10/06/1994
Born: Scotland
Signed: 01/2013

CHLOE LOGAN
Position: Goalkeeper
D.O.B: 19/06/1996
Born: Scotland
Signed: 08/2019

LISA RODGERS
Position: Goalkeeper
D.O.B: 16/02/2006
Born: Scotland
Signed: 01/2024

AMY RICHARDSON
Position: Defender
D.O.B: 05/01/2006
Born: Wales
Signed: 06/2024

CHLOE CRAIG
Position: Defender
D.O.B: 04/09/1993
Born: Scotland
Signed: 01/2009

EMMA LAWTON
Position: Defender
D.O.B: 26/07/2001
Born: Scotland
Signed: 09/2024

NATALIE ROSS
Position: Midfielder
D.O.B: 14/09/1989
Born: Scotland
Signed: 01/2012

JENNY SMITH
Position: Midfielder
D.O.B: 20/06/2002
Born: Scotland
Signed: 06/2023

SHANNON McGREGOR
Position: Midfielder
D.O.B: 07/12/1999
Born: Scotland
Signed: 06/2024

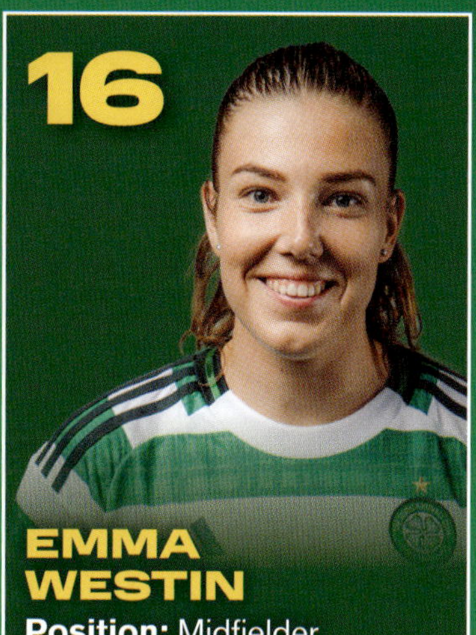

16

EMMA WESTIN
Position: Midfielder
D.O.B: 24/11/1998
Born: Sweden
Signed: 01/2025

25

MOMO NAKAO
Position: Midfielder
D.O.B: 09/03/2002
Born: Japan
Signed: 01/2025

41

CLARE GOLDIE
Position: Midfielder
D.O.B: 05/02/2005
Born: Scotland
Signed: 06/2022

73

MARIA McANENY
Position: Midfielder
D.O.B: 25/06/2004
Born: Scotland
Signed: 06/2021

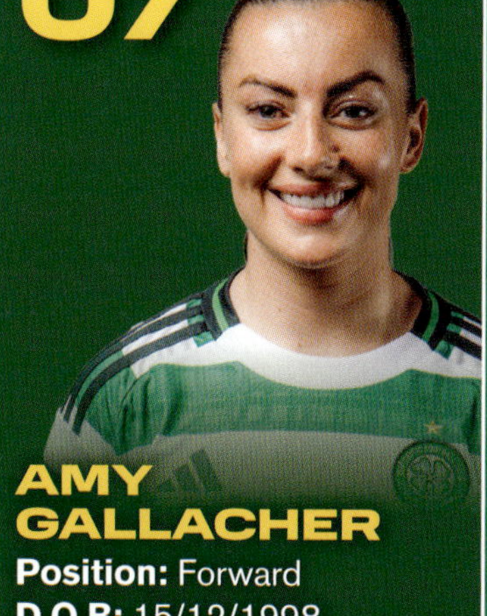

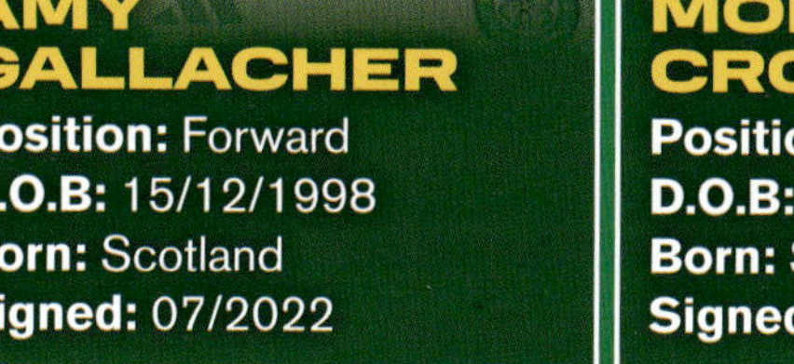

07

AMY GALLACHER
Position: Forward
D.O.B: 15/12/1998
Born: Scotland
Signed: 07/2022

17

MORGAN CROSS
Position: Forward
D.O.B: 12/02/2001
Born: Scotland
Signed: 09/2024

20

SAOIRSE NOONAN
Position: Forward
D.O.B: 13/07/1999
Born: Ireland
Signed: 07/2024

02

CLAIRE WALSH
Position: Defender
D.O.B: 28/10/1994
Born: Ireland
Signed: 07/2025

04

LISA ROBERTSON
Position: Midfielder
D.O.B: 16/05/1992
Born: Scotland
Signed: 01/2020 & 07/2025

46

DARRA DAWSON

Position: Defender
D.O.B: 03/11/2008
Born: Scotland
Signed: 07/2024

47

SIENNA McGOLDRICK

Position: Midfielder
D.O.B: 09/01/2008
Born: Scotland
Signed: 07/2024

33

ADELAIDE GAY

Position: Goalkeeper
D.O.B: 03/11/1989
Born: America
Signed: 08/2025

11

AISLIN STREICEK

Position: Defender
D.O.B: 21/07/2003
Born: Canada
Signed: 08/2025

12

GRACE COURTER

Position: Defender
D.O.B: 09/10/2002
Born: America
Signed: 08/2025

CELTICFCTRAVEL.COM
TRAVEL THE CELTIC WAY
SCOTTISH CHAMPIONS

DOT-TO-DOT

Do you know who this is? Join the dots to reveal the Hoops hero!

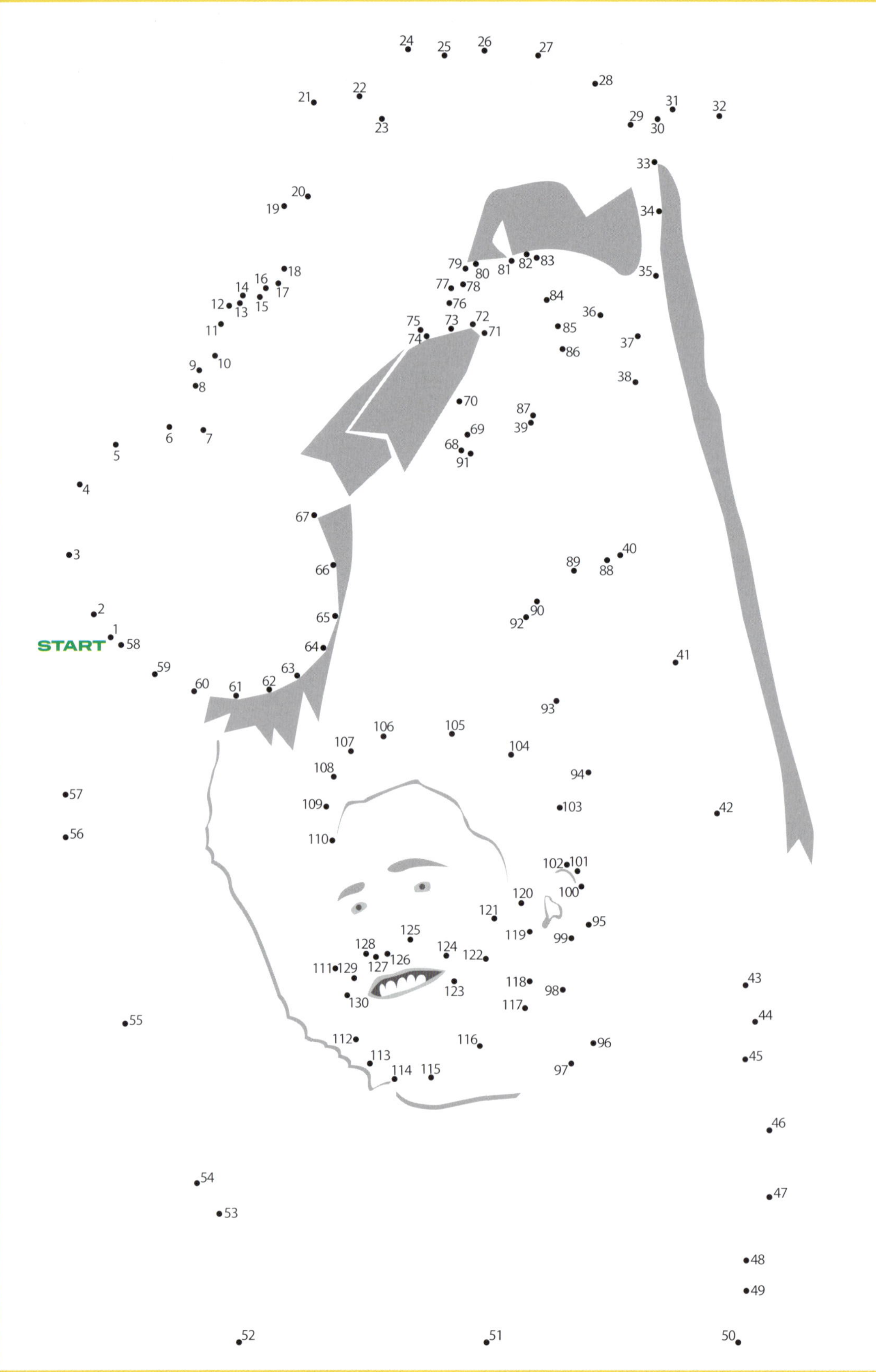

2024/25 QUIZ

Were you paying attention during the season?

1. Let's start at the very beginning, who scored Celtic's first goal of the campaign on Flag Day?

2. Which side did Celtic play in successive games during the season?

3. Jota made a scoring return for the Hoops, but against which side?

4. And what club did he arrive from?

5. Daizen Maeda scored two hat-tricks during the season, in what competitions were they scored?

6. Viljami Sinisalo made his debut against which side?

7. Celtic's highest score of the season was 6-0, but against which two sides?

8. Celtic's first ever opponents in the new-format UEFA Champions League were which team?

9. How many Celts hit double figures in goals over the course of the season?

10. James Forrest famously scored Celtic's final league goal, but who scored the last away goal?

SPOT THE BALL

DAIZEN Maeda is on the run towards goal again in the Trophy Day game against St Mirren, but which is the real ball in this picture?

Answers on pages 62/63.

EMMA LAWTON

GHIRL ON TOP OF HER GAME

SEASON 2024/25 was a bit of a whirlwind for defender Emma Lawton as she went from part-time football with Partick Thistle to playing in the UEFA Women's Champions League with Celtic, gaining her first Scotland cap AND, to put the icing on the cake, winning the PFA Player of the Year award.

As the September 2024 transfer deadline day approached, Lawton was making plans for the next game when Partick Thistle would welcome Celtic, who she played for at Academy level, to the Maryhill club's passing home at the Kirkintilloch Community Sports Complex on Sunday, September 15.

Indeed, the defender did play in the game, but in the Hoops of Celtic as she and Morgan Cross who earlier in the week had been a Motherwell player, both signed for Celtic on the transfer deadline day of Friday, September 13.

Now, Friday the 13th may be held as bad luck for some, but not for Emma Lawton nor Celtic FC Women as she hasn't looked back since then with her performances in a raft of games for the club also being noticed elsewhere – hence the international call-up and the Player of the Year award.

In between playing with the Celtic Academy and returning to sign a three-year deal with the Hoops, two spells at Partick Thistle for Lawton had sandwiched stints at Manchester City and Motherwell, as well as playing friendlies for Scotland at Under-23 level, and, at 23-years-old, she was delighted to return to the Ghirls.

She said when she rejoined the Hoops:

"I'm just delighted to have signed for the club. It's obviously such a huge club, with so much history in recent years.

"So, to be back playing for the club again after coming through the Academy, it's a really proud moment.

"I was obviously here when I was younger playing for a few of the Academy age groups.

"So, to think back then that I could come back here and be a full-time footballer now with Celtic, I probably would never have imagined that.

"So, to be back and to say I'm a full-time footballer, it's a very humbling moment for me and my family.

"I've been at numerous different clubs already. Each one of those moves and time spent there has taught me loads of different things.

"So, hopefully, I can continue taking all those learning points and experiences, then bring them in to Celtic this time."

She certainly did continue with her learning curve, indeed, it took a sharp upwards turn as she transitioned to full-time football training and playing with ease.

And that was reflected with her international call-up and a debut cap in an away UEFA Women's Nations League game against Austria in February 2025, then, just four days later she scored her first international goal in her first Hampden game for the national side.

Then, as a magnificent season for her neared its end, came the honour that was voted for by her fellow SWPL players – the PFA Player of the Year award.

She said on the night:

"I think it's a very special award. It kind of concludes my season quite nicely with how well it has gone for me.

"Getting the PFA award was really special, particularly as it's players within the league voting for you.

"So to get that kind of recognition from the league, it's a really proud moment for me personally.

"I'm kind of one of these players who doesn't usually like an off-season because I just want to play, but I think I will enjoy my time off at the end of the season and it will give me a chance to reflect with my friends and family.

"Then I'll be able to appreciate what I have done this season - signing for Celtic, I couldn't have imagined how it would have gone.

"It's definitely going to be nice to reflect back on it."

B-TEAM BREAK-THROUGH BHOYS

THE YOUNGSTERS WHO MADE THE STEP UP

YOU only have to look at the examples of James Forrest and Callum McGregor, who have won 50 winner's medals between them, to see just what can be achieved by coming through the ranks at the Celtic Youth Academy.

Another long-serving Celt to come through the ranks is Anthony Ralston who is now into his 11th season as a first-team Celt.

For each of these players, their first-team careers started, of course, with their debut – a big day for any young player, and, everyone – coaching staff, team-mates, supporters and, certainly the player himself wondering what this will lead to.

During the course of the 2024/25 season, four Celtic Youth Academy graduates made that step up from Stephen McManus' B team squad to first-team football under Brendan Rodgers.

FRANCIS TURLEY DEBUT DATA

Age: 18 years, 224 days
Position: Midfielder
Date: 25/08/24
Venue: St Mirren Park
Competition: SPFL
Opposition: St Mirren
Score: 3-0

Belfast Bhoy, Francis Turley was the first of the 2024/25 debutants to make an appearance during the season when, in only the third league game of the term, he replaced Reo Hatate in the 89th minute of a 3-0 win over St Mirren. Celtic started well in the Paisley rain with captain Callum McGregor scoring after only three minutes. Hatate added another before the break, and defender Alistair Johnston scored the third and final goal in the 71st minute. Turley, who had performed well and scored in the pre-season win over Queen's Park was given a welcoming ovation by the travelling support.

DANIEL CUMMINGS DEBUT DATA

Age: 18 years and 290 days
Position: Forward
Date: 29/01/25
Venue: Villa Park
Competition: UCL
Opposition: Aston Villa
Score: 2-4

Next up is Daniel Cummings, and the young Glaswegian couldn't have foreseen making his debut amid the glamour of an away game in the Champions League which was also a cross-border trip to England. The final outcome in this league phase game saw Celtic qualify for a play-off tie with Bayern Munich, but they had to settle for a 4-2 defeat to Aston Villa in Birmingham. It was a valiant effort with Adam Idah netting two first-half goals as the teams went in 2-2 at half-time. Indeed it was Idah who was replaced by Cummings in the 79th minute as further Villa goals in the 60th and 91st minutes took the game.

JUDE BONNAR DEBUT DATA

Age: 19 years and 100 days
Position: Midfielder
Date: 25/02/25
Venue: Celtic Park
Competition: SPFL
Opposition: Aberdeen
Score: 5-1

The Celts extended their lead at the top of the table as Hamilton Bhoy, Jude Bonnar made his debut in a 5-1 win over Aberdeen at Celtic Park. Daizen Maeda, Jota and Callum McGregor had the Hoops in the driving seat at half-time with the confidence oozing through the team. Yang made it 4-0 in the 72nd minute and, eight minutes later, young Bonnar replaced Arne Engels, and came on to rousing cheers from the Celtic support. The Dons pulled one back in the 90th minute, but Maeda still had time to reinstate Celtic's four-goal lead in the 92nd minute.

SEAN McARDLE DEBUT DATA

Age: 17 years and 256 days
Position: Midfielder
Date: 10/05/25
Venue: Celtic Park
Competition: SPFL
Opposition: Hibernian
Score: 3-1

The only one of the new batch to add to his debut with another appearance during the season was Sean McArdle who played against Hibernian and then Aberdeen just days apart in the two games before Flag Day. It was a professional performance by the Hoops with goals by Nicolas Kühn and Adam Idah giving a 2-1 half-time lead after Hibernian went in front in the 25th minute. Celtic upped the ante in the 58th minute when Hatate made it 3-1, and, in the 85th minute, McArdle replaced Arne Engels to make his debut. His performance saw him also appear in a 5-1 win at Pittodrie four days later when he came on for Luke McCowan in the 81st minute with the Celts 4-1 ahead at the time before Adam Idah scored the fifth.

SPOT THE DIFFERENCE

THERE are 10 differences between these two photographs of Morgan Cross playing against Chelsea in the UEFA Women's Champions League.

The first one has been circled, but can you spot the rest?

STADIUM ANAGRAM XI

HERE we have a team of anagrams of grounds in Scotland that Celtic have played at.

Can you work out what stadiums these are?

EDITOR TIP

ADORERS TEA

CELTS TAN YE

ANCIENT DA

AD MR MICK RAPID

IT HAIL SMURF LID

MAD NOVELLA

HEAD MP PRANK

IVA OR PATRICK

MP RAN STRIKER

GROANED WALKUPS

SKIPPER ARRIVALS

HERE we have a team of players who signed from other senior clubs and went on to become Celtic captains?

Can you match up the captains and the teams they arrived at Celtic from?

Tom Boyd	Borussia Dortmund
Scott Brown	Ayr United
Neil Lennon	Glentoran
Paul Lambert	Hibernian
Jackie McNamara	Chelsea
Bertie Peacock	Stenhousemuir
Jock Stein	Dunfermline
Willie Lyon	Queen's Park
Charlie Shaw	Leicester City
Willie Cringan	Llanelli
Alec McNair	Queens Park Rangers

Answers on pages 62/63.

COUNTRY GHIRLS

THE CELTS WHO HAVE COME FROM FAR AND WIDE FOR CELTIC FC WOMEN

SO far, players from more than 20 countries around the world have jetted in to ply their trade with Celtic FC Women.

CANADA
Clarissa Larisey, Kylla Sjoman, Aislin Streicek

UNITED STATES
Murphy Agnew, Hana Kerner, Kelsey Daugherty, Kit Loferski, Taylor Otto, Cheyenne Shorts, Mariah Lee, Summer Green, Kelsey Hodges, Jaclyn Poucel, Darcy McFarlane, Indi Cowie, Grace Courter, Adelaide Gay

MEXICO
Pamela Tajonar

GUYANA
Sydney Cummings

ARGENTINA
Luana Muñoz

SWEDEN
Emma Westin

DENMARK
Mathilde Carstens, Signe Carstens, Molli Plasmann

ICELAND
María Catharína Ólafsdóttir Grós

IRELAND
Saoirse Noonan, Claire O'Riordan, Tyler Toland, Izzy Atkinson, Caitlin Hayes, Keeva Keenan, Kerry Montgomery, Rebecca Bisland

ENGLAND
Lucy Ashworth-Clifford, Natasha Flint, Charlie Wellings, Danielle Cox

WALES
Amy Richardson, Anna Filbey

FRANCE
Célya Barclais

SPAIN
Paula Partido, Anita Marcos

PORTUGAL
Bruna Lourenço

MOROCCO
Nour Imane Addi

GERMANY
Josephine Giard

MALTA
Anna Vincenti

From all over Europe, to as far afield as China, Japan, Australia and New Zealand at one end of the globe, to Canada, the USA, Mexico and Argentina at the other.

Nigh on 50 non-Scots have made their way to Celtic FC Women, meaning the team's results have been avidly waited for around the world.

The first non-Scot was English-born Republic of Ireland internationalist, Rebecca Bisland when Celtic FC Women took off in 2007, but the vast majority have been this decade.

Among them have been the likes of United States-born attacking midfielder, Indi Cowie back in 2010, she is now a champion freestyler and coach, and the list goes right through to the current side when Momo Nakao became the first player to join the side from Japan.

Here we pinpoint just exactly where in the world the Ghirls came from.

JAPAN
Momo Nakao

CHINA
Shen Mengyu,
Shen Menglu

AUSTRALIA
Jacynta Galabadaarachchi

NEW ZEALAND
Olivia Chance

EVERGREEN CELTS

THE ONE-CLUB PLAYERS WHO HAVE WORN ONLY THE GREEN AND WHITE

WITH nigh on 1,000 Celts having played first-team games for the club over the past 137 years, many of those being dyed-in-the-wool Celtic supporters, you'd be forgiven for thinking that, even in each generation there must be quite a few who played for the Hoops and ONLY the Hoops.

True, many joined the club from other teams, others came through the ranks here but moved on to other clubs for many and varied reasons, and some returned.

Then there are those who departed in the autumn of their career, such as Danny McGrain, who played for a season with Hamilton Accies after finishing with the Celts, or Lisbon Lion, Bobby Lennox who moved to the States in the spring of 1978 and played with Houston Hurricane, and by September he was back at Celtic under new manager, Billy McNeill.

Careers like all of the above are in the vast majority, though, for from that army of players who have represented the club only SIX have been with Celtic throughout their entire career.

That number includes current Celt, James Forrest, who, obviously could move on to another club before retiring, but let's just say that the need for top players to keep on playing has diminished, and we want to see the winger carry on at the Celts in any case.

Here, we take a short look at the careers of those who joined the club as youngsters and stayed until they hung up their boots.

JIMMY QUINN

Age on Debut:
22 years 195 days

1901 to 1915:
331 games 217 goals

The Mighty Quinn is a giant of Celtic's history and scored on his debut in 1901 in a 4-3 win over St Mirren in Paisley. That was a sign of things for the Croy Bhoy who signed from Smithston Albion and became one of the most inspiring Celts ever in driving the team on to grab victory from the jaws of defeat. Perhaps his most famous moment ever was in the Scottish Cup final of 1904, the first in which Celtic wore the Hoops, when the Celts were down 2-0 to Rangers. He grabbed the game by the scruff of the neck and scored a hat-trick in a famous 3-2 win for Celtic. Quinn retired in 1915 and became a regular at Celtic Park along with his fellow Hoops supporters.

CHIC GEATONS

Age on Debut:
21 years 20 days

1929 to 1940:
319 games 11 goals

A Fife Bhoy who played with hometown side, Lochgelly Celtic before making the move through to Glasgow in 1927 as a youngster. The right-half made his debut in the right-back position in 1929 before becoming a star of the 1930s and playing his part in both the sadness and joy of that pre-war decade. It was Geatons who took over in goal in 1931 when Johnny Thomson was fatally injured at Ibrox, and he was also part of the team that lifted the Exhibition Cup in 1938. On retiring in 1941, Geatons held a number of coaching roles at Celtic Park until 1950.

BILLY McNEILL

Age on Debut:

18 years 174 days

1957 to 1975:

790 games 35 goals

The longest-serving among our first-teamers here and Cesar retired at the top with his final game being the 1975 Scottish Cup final win over Airdrie. That took McNeill to 23 top class medals including the European Cup victory at Lisbon in 1967 when Celtic became the first non-Latin team to lift the trophy. The iconic sight of McNeill lifting a trophy was part of being a Celtic supporter in the 1960s and '70s and that carried on during his two spells as manager, including two legendary triumphs in the 4-2 game of 1979 and the Centenary Double in 1988.

PACKIE BONNER

Age on Debut:

18 years 297 days

1979 to 1995:

641 games 0 goals

When an Irishman makes his Celtic debut on St Patrick's Day you can only hope that's a sign of good fortune. And that's exactly what it was when the teenage Pat Bonner played his first Hoops game in 1979 – over a decade-and-a-half later he was still a Celtic goalkeeper and one of the most treasured keepers in the history of the club. Another who went out at the top with a Scottish Cup final win, and, like Billy McNeill before him, it was also against Airdrie, although 20 years later. The only non-Scot in our Evergreen Celts, like the other five, Bonner, played for his country, but thanks to his World Cup heroics in 1990, he truly was a national hero back home in Ireland.

PAUL McSTAY

Age on Debut:

17 years 100 days

1982 to 1997:

677 games 72 goals

Without doubt the finest footballer of our half-dozen Evergreen Celts, and, as well as being the youngest debutant amongst the group, he immediately became a first-team regular at that age becoming one of the most faithful servants the club has ever had. Coming from a family steeped in playing for Celtic since the 1920s, McStay came through the ranks at the club and spent little time in the reserves – very little. The Maestro was a star of the 1980s including the Centenary Year and captained the club during the early '90s – without McStay in the side they would have been even more barren and forgettable than they were.

JAMES FORREST

Age on Debut:

18 years 298 days

2010 to date:

528 games 109 goals
(Stats to end of 2024/25 season)

In an age of agents and transfer windows and all that comes from that, the chances of a player being with one club for their entire career are very limited. So, stand up James Forrest – 26 winner's medals as the most decorated Celt of all time as well as scoring in every one of the past 16 seasons. Athletic Bilbao annually present the One Club Award to players from around the world who have achieved such status, and in 2019 it was awarded to Billy McNeill. So, it was fitting that when James Forrest was rewarded with a testimonial for Celtic, it was Athletic who provided the opposition.

COLOURING-IN

Time to get the crayons, paints or ink markers out and colour in this picture of Celtic FC Women's captain, Kelly Clark.

GUESS WHO?

MAZE

Can you get the players' families and friends down to the pitch to celebrate with the trophy?

Answers on pages 62/63.

IRISH EYES ON THE GOAL

SAOIRSE NOONAN'S GOALDEN SUCCESS

AT the start of last season, Republic of Ireland internationalist, Saoirse Noonan became Elena Sadiku's sixth new signing of the transfer window when she put pen to paper on a three-year-deal with the Hoops.

And it proved to be a shrewd move by the Swedish head coach as the 31 goals scored by the striker topped the scoring charts with the Celts.

The Cork Ghirl, played youth level with Kilreen Celtic and Douglas Hall AFC as well as also being very successful in Gaelic football as a youngster with Nemo Rangers.

Her senior career started with hometown side Cork City in 2015 and she moved to Dublin six years later with Shelbourne. It was only then that she gave up GAA to focus purely on football and that was rewarded with a move over the water to Durham in 2022.

There was a loan spell back at Shelbourne while recovering from a knee injury, but on her return to Durham, she played out until 2024 when Celtic swooped.

Arriving at Celtic, Noonan said: "It's a bit surreal for me. I was a Celtic fan growing up and all my family are Celtic fans. I can't wait to get going.

"I thought I'd never get over here, so I'm delighted to be here now.

"I grew up playing on the streets and went to Cork City and then to Shelbourne. Then I crossed the water to Durham.

"Now I've made the move up here to Scotland to Celtic. Celtic's a huge club and I'm delighted to be a part of it now."

And she had European football to look forward to, saying: "It's the highest level you can play at in club football. To wear the Celtic jersey and go out and play at that level is something any young kid aspires to.

"Seeing the girls win the league and going on to play in the Champions League, it's something I've always dreamed of. It's everyone's dream and it's something that I can't wait to do.

"It's been really positive from the get-go. Elena showed belief in me, she told me aspects she can see that I can improve and get in to the team.

"I'm Irish. I play with my heart on my sleeve. I bleed green. I'll give my all, work as hard as I can and hopefully get plenty of goals."

Noonan did, indeed get plenty of goals in the Hoops, and those 31 goals, of course, automatically won her the club's Women's Top Goalscorer of the Year award at the annual Celtic Player of the Year Awards ceremony when the event was held at the Doubletree By Hilton Glasgow Central in the city in May.

It was a night of sparkling success as she shared the stage with Daizen Maeda who had just picked up the same award for the men's team.

It was something Noonan may barely have envisaged when she signed for Celtic back at the start of the term as the building process went on in the women's team.

Another dream of hers was to get back into the Republic of Ireland team. After playing her way through the national age ranks, Noonan had three senior caps by the time she joined Celtic, but she hadn't played for her country since 2023.

That was rectified at the end of March last year when manager Carla Ward called Noonan up to the squad.

Noonan said of the news: "I'm delighted to have received the call-up. I think it's every player's ambition and dream to play for their country. So, I'm absolutely over the moon.

"I got a text from Carla, just asking for a phone call. So, I obviously got back to her right away and had to wait a while until she was free.

"But I was unsure what the outcome of the call might be, so it was just a case of waiting and seeing. So, when they told me, I was absolutely delighted.

"It's been some time now since I was called up. I think my last cap was 2023 against Zambia, before the World Cup.

"So, I think as a player and a person I have grown in both aspects. So, I definitely think I have an older head on my shoulders now and I can go in and try to grab the opportunity with both hands.

"I'm going into camp on good form, with a few goals behind me. So, I'm just going to keep trying to do what I do for Celtic.

"If I was able to get the goal then that would be the icing on the cake really."

In the UEFA Women's Nations League, Noonan played in 2-1 and 4-0 wins over Greece, but that icing on the cake finally did come, and it came on home ground in Cork of all places at the SuperValu Páirc Uí Chaoimh.

On June 3 2025, with the Irish needing a win over Slovenia to finish second in their group and go into a two-legged play-off, in the 19th minute, with a looping header, Noonan scored the only goal of the game in front of nearly 10,000 fans at the same ground where the men's team would play later that summer.

THE GOALS

Opponent	Goals
Dundee United	2
Motherwell	1
KuPS	3
Montrose	3
Montrose	3
Rangers	1
Motherwell	1
Rangers	1
Montrose	3
Spartans	2
Partick Thistle	2
Aberdeen	2
Hearts	1
Queen's Park	2
Hearts	1
Glasgow City	1
Hibernian	1
Motherwell	1
TOTAL	31

HATS OFF TO SAOIRSE

SAOIRSE NOONAN'S 31-goal tally comes from nine singles, five doubles and no fewer than four hat-tricks.

And we have to wonder what the striker has against Montrose as, after scoring a triple against KuPS on European duty, she netted a hat-trick of hat-tricks against the Links Park club.

The first came away in a 4-2 away win in the league in September, then 10 days later following two UEFA Women's Champions League qualifiers, Celtic's very next domestic game was in the League Cup at the same Angus venue, and this time Noonan's hat-trick helped Celtic to a 7-0 win over Montrose.

The final triple came in the return league game at New Douglas Park in November when the Irish striker scored three of the Celtic goals in a 5-1 win.

All she would say was: "It's always nice to score as a striker. At the end of the day, that is part of my job. But credit has to go to all the girls."

DOUBLE FIGURES FOR BRENDAN

LEAGUE CUP WIN IS MANAGER'S 10TH TROPHY SUCCESS

League Cup final
Sunday, December 15, 2024, Hampden Park, Glasgow

CELTIC 3	RANGERS 3
(Taylor 56, Maeda 60, Kühn 87)	(Bajrami 41, Diomande 75, Danilo 88)

Celtic win 5-4 on penalties

CELTIC experienced both sides of the penalty shoot-out scenario at Hampden during the 2024/25 season, and the first was by far the more enjoyable – not that you could ever say that about shoot-outs while they are underway.

The first tournament of the season, the League Cup was up for grabs, with the silverware accompanying the psychological impact and bragging rights that come with winning a trophy in the first half of the term against your city rivals.

The game delivered a thrilling 90 minutes that saw both sides score three goals each – with one coming for each team in the 87th and 88th minutes.

That was still the score on the big screen as the final whistle went at the end of extra time, and the capacity crowd steadied themselves for what was to come, but only one end would be celebrating at the end.

Shooting into the Mount Florida End, successful penalties from Adam Idah, Callum McGregor, Arne Engels and Reo Hatate, along with Kasper Schmeichel's penalty save set the stage for Daizen Maeda to step forward and fire home the winning penalty, giving Brendan Rodgers his 10th trophy as Celtic manager.

As well as being the manager's 10th trophy, the League Cup was also the first trophy won by Brendan Rodgers back in 2016/17, and that was also the club's 100th trophy win – given that this 2024 win was Celtic's 119th major success and that tally would be 120 by the end of the term is truly a mark of the Hoops' dominance in the intervening years.

ONE, TWO, THREE, FOUR, FIVE-NIL

THE MANAGER'S QUADRUPLE FIVE-STAR TITLE SUCCESSES

CELTIC manager, Brendan Rodgers has won each of the four SPFL titles he has competed for, and, amazingly, every one of the four championships was clinched with a 5-0 win.

His first two were successive titles in his first spell with the club, while he has mirrored that with consecutive championships in his first two seasons of his current spell – 2016/17, 2017/18, 2023/24 and 2024/25 being the successes.

The titles have all been sealed against four different clubs at four different grounds, with the second of those being the only clincher at Celtic Park.

James Forrest and Callum McGregor are the only Celts to play in all four games, and both scored in the only one sealed at Paradise.

Here we take a look back at the four title-winning games that had a 20-0 aggregate score.

Scottish Premiership, Sunday, April 2, 2017, Tynecastle Stadium, Edinburgh

HEARTS... 0

CELTIC... 5
(Sinclair 24, 27 & 84 (pen), Armstrong 55, Roberts 61)

Celtic started their league campaign at Tynecastle with a win in Brendan Rodgers' first domestic game in charge, in what was to prove to be the Invincible season and this title win being the second of the Treble in his first season. It was also a title that saw Scott Brown become the first Celt to be a league winner under four different managers. In his first game, Scott Sinclair famously scored at Tynecastle that started the Invincible run, and he scored a hat-trick in this 5-0 win with Stuart Armstrong and Patrick Roberts adding to the score on a day to remember in the capital. This was also the third time in the club's history that the team had achieved six-in-a-row.

Scottish Premiership, Sunday, April 29, 2018, Celtic Park, Glasgow

CELTIC... 5
(Edouard 14 & 41, Forrest 45, Rogic 47, McGregor 53)

RANGERS... 0

The only game of the four to have been played at Celtic Park, and what a game it turned out to be as the Hoops tore Rangers apart in an arresting display in which Mikael Lustig could even take time out to do some policing duties – one of Glasgow's finest joining Glasgow's finest. The Swede's donning of a police cap and taking up the moniker of PC Lustig came in the celebrations following a truly incredibly goal by James Forrest. That was the third goal in the game which also saw an Odsonne Edouard double and a goal by Tom Rogic, while it was Callum McGregor's strike that took us to the required 5-0 tally for this feature.

THREE

Scottish Premiership, Wednesday, May 15, 2024, Rugby Park, Kilmarnock

KILMARNOCK... 0

CELTIC... 5
(Idah 5, Maeda 12, Forrest 35, O'Riley 51 & 71)

Prior to kick-off, the fans and players of both clubs marked the 16th anniversary of the passing of the legendary Tommy Burns with a minute's applause. It didn't take long for Celtic to tighten their grasp on the trophy as Adam Idah and Daizen Maeda had the side 2-0 ahead by the 12th minute. It was 3-0 by half-time thanks to another goal by James Forrest as fans around the world began to party early. Matt O'Riley struck twice in the second half for the 5-0 win and the fans then celebrated in earnest, and, when Brendan Rodgers arrived with the team back at Celtic Park when midnight approached, there were still thousands of supporters lining The Celtic Way to welcome the Champions and the title home.

FOUR

Scottish Premiership, Saturday, April 26, 2025, Tannadice Park, Dundee

DUNDEE UNITED...0

CELTIC...5
(Strain 30 (og), Kühn 38 & 45+3, Idah 47 & 58)

This was the day when four-in-a-row for Celtic, and another type of four-in-a-row for Brendan Rodgers was achieved with a win at Tannadice. The title-clincher came courtesy of an emphatic 5-0 win over Dundee United which also ensured that James Forrest became Celtic's most decorated player with his 26th top-class win. Those 26 wins also helped take the club to their 120th trophy victory in a 5-0 scoreline which started with an own goal from the home side. It was then left to Nicolas Kühn and Adam Idah to come up with doubles as highlights of Brendan Rodgers' fourth title won with a fourth 5-0 victory.

ANSWERS

P42 DOT-TO-DOT

It's keeper, **Kasper Schmeichel** with the SPFL trophy.

P43 2024/25 QUIZ

Were you paying attention during the season, here are the answers.

1. **Reo Hatate**
2. **Hibernian**
3. **Motherwell**
4. **Rennes**
5. **League Cup and Scottish Cup**
6. **Raith Rovers**
7. **Aberdeen and Dundee**
8. **Slovan Bratislava**
9. **Seven**
10. **Adam Idah**

SPOT THE BALL

Here is the real ball **C**.

P48 SPOT THE DIFFERENCE